The Entrepreneur Paradox

The Easy Way To Achieve
Balance And Wealth

Sandro Heitor

The Entrepreneur Paradox

The Easy Way To Achieve Balance And Wealth

Copyright © 2019 Sandro Heitor

All rights reserved. No part of this document may be reproduced or transmitted in any form whatsoever, electronic, or mechanical, including photocopying, recording, or by any informational storage or retrieval system of any nature without the express written, dated and signed permission of the author.

ISBN: 9781095358948

Book Design & Book Writing Coaching & Publishing done with the help of:
Lily Patrascu
Brand for Speakers
www.brandforspeakers.com

Limits of liability / disclaimer of warranty: The author and publisher of this book have used their best efforts in preparing this material. The author and publisher make no representation or warranties with respect to the accuracy, applicability, or completeness of the contents. They disclaim any warranties (express or implied), merchantability for any particular purpose. The author and publisher shall in no event be held liable for any loss or other damages, including but not limited to special, incidental, consequential, or other damages. The information presented in this publication is compiled from sources believed to be accurate; however, the publishers assume no responsibility for errors or omissions. The information in this publication is not intended to replace or substitute professional advice. The author and publisher specifically disclaim any liability, loss, or risk that is incurred as a consequence, directly or indirectly, of the use and application of any of the contents of this work.

TABLE OF CONTENTS

Praise For The Book..5
Foreword By Harry Sardinas..................................9
About The Book..13
About The Author...15
Note To The Reader...25
Acknowledgements..26
Chapter 1: The Entrepreneur Paradox System.................27
Chapter 2: Find Your Happiness..............................31
Chapter 3: Find Your Life Purpose..........................46
Chapter 4: Assess How Fulfilled You Are.................55
Chapter 5: Seek Financial, Time And Choice Freedom.......69
Chapter 6: Contribute To The Universe....................75
Chapter 7: Be Aware Of Potential Improvement..........81
Chapter 8: The More You Fail, The Closer You Are To Success..99
Chapter 9: Identify Your Talents.............................124
Chapter 10: How To Build On Your Belief................131
Chapter 11: How To Stay Consistent........................142

Chapter 12: How To Achieve Physical Balance.................148

Chapter 13: Achieve Emotional Balance Through Stillness And Meditation..156

Chapter 14: Reward Yourself....................................161

Summary..169

Praise For The Book

"As an entrepreneur, it is often difficult to have balance. In fact, I gave up a long time ago the idea of having balance. I am an empowerment, leadership and public speaking coach and I am so driven and passionate about empowering people that I don't feel I am working at all, regardless of the number of hours worked.

This book inspired me to believe that it is actually possible to build a great business that makes a difference and also take time to retreat, have fun and have a bit more balance to enhance productivity. Sandro has shown in this book that it is really possible to achieve this. Look forward to implement the advice in this book. Highly recommended!"

Harry Sardinas, www.SpeakersAreLeaders.com, Empowerment, Leadership And Public Speaking Coach.

"Entrepreneur Sandro Heitor shares his story and secrets of how he has taken the experiences the many lessons in his life, both positive and negative, and learned from them to grow and master himself.

Life is a journey and we can many times get swallowed up or learn to ride the wave and enjoy the journey so we can experience and trust the flow and our internal compass.

Sandro's story shows us that, no matter where we come from or what we experience in life, we have the ability to overcome, once we are able to go within and connect with ourselves on all levels: physical, mental, emotional and spiritual. Once we can find the inner essence and power of who we truly are and master the flow of spiritual and physical, we can, indeed, have true fulfillment and joy, each and every day of our lives.

I invite you to do as Sandro has done and find the real true YOU, allow yourself to live in the present moment each and every day, and know that all you need to master yourself and achieve your success for YOU in YOUR life is inside of you."

Martina Coogan, CEO of The Mystery School Europe, www.MartinaCoogan.com

---

"This book explains the basic concept of creating wealth and abundance in one's life. Sandro shared his personal journey of how he built a successful business by maintaining balance in the mental, physical and spiritual aspects of his life. As a property investor, I can relate to the three principles mentioned in the book; I likened them to a tripod, which can only maintain balance with the help of the three legs. Taking off even a single leg leads to the tripod losing stability.

This book has inspired me to make sure I balance all aspects of my life and I also understood why many businesses are not succeeding. The quickest way to learn is by learning from those who have been on the journey and achieved success. Sandro has given us a path to follow by writing this book.
If you are planning on starting your own business or you are already in business, I invite you to read this book, for it's a blueprint for building a

sustainable business. Thanks, Sandro, for inspiring us with this book, as I have identified the areas I need to work on in my own life and business."

Aminu Ahmadu
Property Investor; Co-founder Niam Asset

Foreword By Harry Sardinas
Public Speaking, Empowerment and Leadership Coach

Sandro Heitor is a young property investor and property developer with amazing drive and extraordinary results.

I am inspired and astonished by his enthusiasm, energy, and what he managed to achieve in a relatively short space of time. He shares the incredible strategies for building an ultra-successful property development business in this transformational book.

As an empowerment, public speaking and leadership coach, I come across thousands of people who try to build a successful business.

The thing that separates Sandro from many entrepreneurs who fail is his commitment and his incredible drive and passion in the face of multiple challenges and obstacles.

Sandro shares in this book some ultra-important elements, often overlooked, which constitute his secret sauce for attracting the right people in his life at the right time, even at a time when he had almost given up on himself.
Sandro has a quality not many people have – the ability to do things now and work things out later, trusting in the process and knowing in his heart everything will work out.

This is something not many people are willing to do, because they are held back by the thought of being criticised or being judged.

During the Speakers are Leaders workshop, I surprised him and asked him to lead the speaker training exercises, and he didn't hesitate, despite never having spoken in front of groups before. As a result, he is now starting his own podcast and I am certain he is going to build a huge following because he is passionate about the information in this book.

Entrepreneurship is not for the faint-hearted. Sandro shares a blueprint for achieving balance so that you, too, can achieve a successful business, as he has managed to do.

I have personally benefited from the advice in his book, since I rarely take time to completely switch off and retreat or meditate, which has an impact on my work.

He has inspired me to get back in shape and he has made me realise how important balance really is to yield the best results.

A GUIDEBOOK TO MAKING IT BIG!
CLIMBING
BIG
BEN
HOW TO SURVIVE, THRIVE AND SUCCEED
IN LONDON
HARRY SARDINAS
CLIMBING BIG BEN
HARRY SARDINAS

Speakers Are Leaders
Empower Yourself To Start Your Speaking Career
Harry Sardinas & Lily Patrascu
SPEAKERS ARE LEADERS
Harry Sardinas & Lily Patrascu

About The Book

You are not alone. Why is it that a massive percentage of individuals who achieve success are not happy or have a fulfilment that does not last?

The intention of this book is to share the journey of a path of discovery which we will all undertake the moment we decide to take control of our lives and live our dream life. The journey will not define who you are, but it will turn you into the person you want to become.

The journey of an entrepreneur – or anyone who wants to change their life – will be beset with many challenges. It all depends on the "size" of the change or the size of the "dream" you want.

It is a journey that will not give you many validations or significance along the way, because before achieving, you are giving, filtering through the crowd, navigating between trial and error.

Mentally, physically and spiritually, we are walking down a path we have not been taught how to cope and deal with, let alone understand. If that's you, I want you to know you are not alone. All this is normal and part of the journey. Years ago, I was just like you, looking for my own path and my purpose.

I intend to assure you that there is no other way to become a successful entrepreneur but to take the path full of roadblocks, obstacles and challenges. All that is part of the journey towards having the wealth, the fulfilment and anything you desire. I am intending this to be a blueprint for your success, so you don't need to struggle like I did for many years.

They say information is "power". Well, this is my intention: to share information that this journey is the only way to achieve, transform, build the life of your dreams and to do so with belief, trust, consciousness and balance, so you can have a smoother ride to success.

Nothing is worth achieving if you are not taking care of yourself as a whole – your mind, body and spirit.

About The Author

Sandro Heitor went from being homeless at the young age of four years old to creating a property development empire, thanks to his enormous drive, passion and an entrepreneurial spirit.

He continued working through enormous challenges and going through multiple unfulfilling low-paid jobs, until he finally realised the source of his success was not chasing money, but bettering himself.

He went on a spiritual quest and learned to understand the power of being LOVE and living the full meaning of it in his life, which enabled him to overcome his pride, accept his self-worth, identify his talents and accept failure as being an inevitable part of the process of succeeding.

He started a process of personal development, by focusing on finding his true passion and purpose, and seeking a solution for his obstacles.

His experience as a receptionist for a medical practice helped him develop compassion for and acceptance of others, which would come in handy later in his property success.

His work in accounts for a fine art publisher enabled him to become financially literate. He went on to work for a private equity firm, then a property company, selling property investments. There, he finally discovered his knack for entrepreneurship, through collaborating successfully with others, and he is now achieving the vision he had to build 22 units in London this year alone.

It was only when he started implementing true balance in his life, despite all the hardships that came his way, that he started to attract the right people in his life – people that complemented his skills and led him to success.

It was only when he focused on being happy, and balanced mentally, physically, and spiritually, that he started to see results and stopped spinning his wheels, trying to succeed.

He is now happy because he is using his property business to create positive outcomes for other people, and he is feeling much more confident than in the past in all areas of his life.

He now wants to empower you, and thousands of other people who are trapped in the vicious circle of the rat race; this is for you, if you are someone who feels you have no way out.

Sandro's message is that, wherever you are in your life right now, there is another way. It may feel life is tough sometimes, but it is only this way because it is meant to make you feel stronger and empower you to live the life you really want to live.

My Story

Imagine a tiny, timid, four-year-old Portuguese boy in dirty hand-me-down clothes and ripped shoes, on a cold winter's day in London, in 1990.
That little boy was me.

I was homeless, sleeping on the streets of London with my mum and dad, in churches, office spaces, or wherever we could find, until we could afford to find a room. My parents would drag me from place to place and I would follow them, hopelessly. Life had taken to beating me at a very young age.

We called ourselves "the trio".

We hung out together, looking desperately for a better life in the UK – which was meant to be the Holy Grail of opportunities. For a long time, it didn't feel that way. We were frozen on the streets of London, feeling stuck. My parents were trying really hard to give me the best they could. And, at least, we were together.

We eventually found a "room" above a fish and chip shop. As I entered the fish and chip shop for the first time, the smell hit me in the face. It was a penetrating smell that would permeate all my clothes. But it was food. I was overjoyed at the sight of chips, until I realised my mum didn't have enough money to buy a Coca-Cola, too.

It was the first time I felt rejection, embarrassment, a feeling of not being enough — all in the same conversation. In the face of awkwardness, I was adamant that I wanted the drink, too.

It was the first time I felt the impact of extreme kindness from someone I had never met before. After a conversation in broken English, the owner of the shop gave us not one, but three, cans of Coca-Cola.

The memory of this experience touched me at one of my lowest moments on the journey to success, and changed my life. In that moment, I made a decision to dream BIG and to do whatever it took to have an IMPACT on others, just like the fish and chip shop owner had an impact on me.

By the age of 16, there had already been enough subconscious experiences to make me decide to want to have my own business, to manage my own time, and to be in control of my own life.

Seeing my parents work from 5.30 a.m. to 8 p.m., day after day, made me take a subconscious decision that I had to make a difference, in my life and theirs.

As time went on, property became a subject. For four years, from the age of 16, I was in the company of an individual who instilled property in me. After pursuing this between the ages of 16 and 21, I still could not get on the property ladder. It felt like I was spinning my wheels, getting nowhere. The harder I tried to chase money, the further money seemed to stay away from me.

I worked in accounts for a fine art publisher in London, after one year in the same company doing the tedious work of copying and pasting jpeg images from a CD.

At the age of 22, I started travelling. I saw the opportunity of buying abroad and, once I got back to London and did some research, my two best friends and I stumbled upon a London property course, which we signed up to. Six months later, I bought my first property and the journey began.

Within 12 months, in 2010, we owned two properties in London and rented them out as room lets. We saw the potential, but we knew the dream was bigger than just buying and renting.

In May 2010 I handed in my notice, intending to jump ship and take property seriously. I had been headhunted by a company that turned out to be a fraud. Frustration mounted as, three months after leaving my full-time job, I was still unemployed.

Two months after that, I joined a property investment company selling properties all over London, where I learnt the processes for packaging investments. However, I was made redundant within 12 months.
I made the decision, then, to dedicate all my time to my new company, called Trio. That was in October 2011.

Between May 2010 and February 2015, I had no financial stability. The only thing that kept me going was my drive to succeed, the belief that I was capable and an unexplainable feeling of knowing I was going to be alright.

Since 2015, I have finally started to see the light at the end of the tunnel because I became better and more confident in all areas of my life. I started going to the gym, committing to my physical body because I was looking for a way to release the physical and mental pressure that was building during the week in my business.

I started realising the impact of aligning my mind, body and spirit, through taking time to walk in nature, reflect and meditate, so that I could take better decisions at work and be less reactive to what was going on.

I started paying better attention to my nutrition and took time to connect spiritually, which enabled me to raise my energy and become a magnetic entrepreneur, which meant I was attracting opportunities, people, situations, things, everything I really wanted, to me. Rather than having to work hard, I was now working smart, on my terms.

Since then, I have been in flow.

Becoming an author and a speaker was something that was on my list two years ago. I thought I could potentially achieve it by the time I was 50 years old. But here is the book I wrote, in your hands or within your reach, now, 18 years sooner than expected.

The entrepreneur paradox is that we are trained to believe that all we have to do is to take action, be driven and keep going, and eventually we will succeed. We are trained to believe that hard work gets results. The truth is that hard work is only a part of what is required in the successful entrepreneur's journey.

The reality is that when you create balance in your mind, body and spirit, you create endless opportunities for yourself. You activate the laws of attraction. The Universe starts collaborating with you. High-end clients are attracted to your energy and enthusiasm, regardless of how much money you have in your pocket.

The entrepreneur paradox is that when you chase money, you are hit by obstacles. It feels hard getting clients. When you chase money, you are in an eternal circle looking for the next opportunity, that may or may not work for you.

However, when you start focusing on your personal growth and on mental, emotional, spiritual and body alignment, on enhancing your energy, you get happiness, fulfilment, wealth, abundance and joy.

You also become a magnetic entrepreneur who attracts everything you could possibly want in your life.

I have used this blueprint for success to go from zero to building a successful property development business and I now would like to share my message to help you, too, in the same way that I was given help in my most desperate moments.

I am now an ambitious, driven, and self-taught individual who believes in doing and being better, every day. One of the keys to my success is keeping going in the face of adversity, a "can do" attitude, and developing my empathic energy to connect with people from all walks of life.

Note To The Reader

Dear Reader,

You may have picked up this book because you are an entrepreneur or you want to be one. Either way, I feel nothing in this life happens by accident. There is a special reason why you picked this book out of the millions of books available.

The Universe is clearly collaborating to help you achieve your goals. I hope you will make the most of it. It really condenses my blood, sweat and tears into the blueprint I created to give you a shortcut to success and not have to struggle, the way I did.

When you implement the system I created, you will realise there is a better way to have the same entrepreneurial journey with bigger success and less hassle.

Hope to meet you someday,

Sandro

Acknowledgements

Thank you to Lily Patrascu for helping me get this book branded and published. It made my dream come true to have it done so much quicker than I expected.
Thank you to Harry Sardinas for believing in me and inviting me to your Speakers Are Leaders programme, which enabled me to become a powerful speaker much faster than I ever imagined possible.

Thank you to my family for being my rock.

Thank you to Hugo Fonseca and Ricardo Oliveira, for always believing in and supporting me as a business partner. We complement each other so well.

A massive thank you to Daniel Toledo for being my personal trainer and nutritionist. You keep my fitness levels high and mental focus strong.

Chapter 1
The Entrepreneur Paradox System

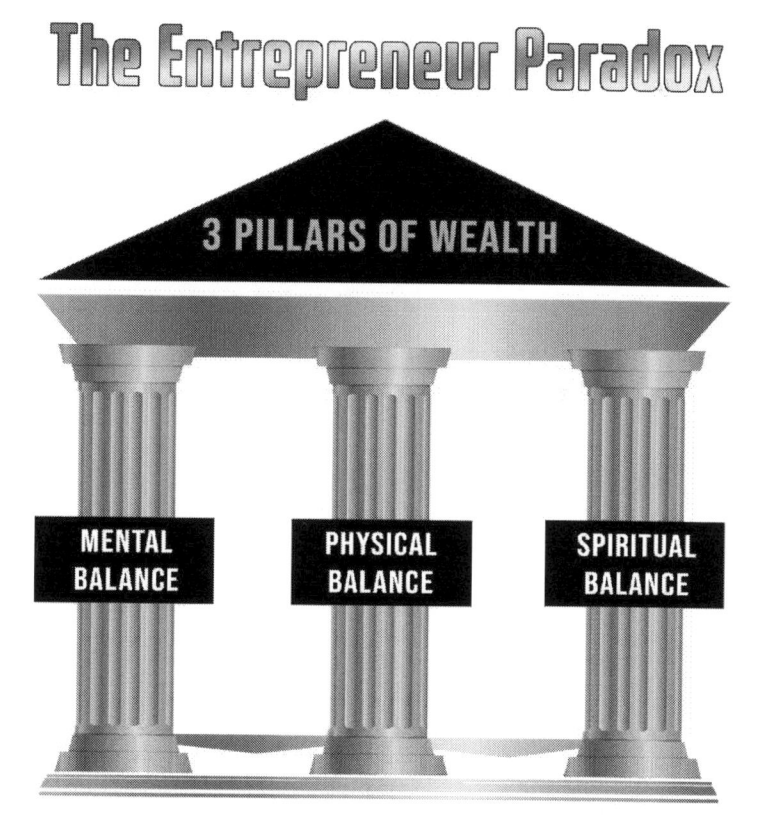

The Entrepreneur Paradox

3 PILLARS OF WEALTH

MENTAL BALANCE | PHYSICAL BALANCE | SPIRITUAL BALANCE

What is the Entrepreneur Paradox?

The Entrepreneur Paradox is that, as entrepreneurs, we focus on creating wealth on an imbalanced foundation. We spin our wheels, we try harder and harder, and even harder.

We chase money, we chase clients, instead of focusing on making a difference or solving a problem for others.

We chase money and we are surprised when money runs away from us even faster.

We are then surprised to see how we fail.

We are surprised to see how apparently highly successful people who have attained recognition and wealth, and who appear to have everything they desire, kill themselves or have a life they simply don't enjoy.

Through my own entrepreneurial journey I discovered there is a better way – it is called BALANCE.

Balance may seem hard but the reality is that unless you take the time to create balance, unless you take the time to work on yourself physically, spiritually, mentally, you are building on a foundation that could collapse at any time.

That is why I created the Entrepreneur Paradox system. It is made up of three pillars of wealth: the mental balance, the physical balance and the spiritual balance.

I am not saying that these are the only elements required to build a solid foundation for a business, but I am saying that these are critical elements that need to be there before you start looking for finance, looking for investors, looking for clients, making sales, creating a marketing plan, etc.

Balance is needed in your life so that you can have the ability to bounce back from any difficult situation, failure, obstacle or any other event or situation blocking your progress as an entrepreneur.

As you are building your business from scratch, you need to remain balanced. Lack of balance will have consequences at the worst possible moments.

You also need to take yourself out of the way. Building a business is not about you. It is about what your clients need and want. When you focus on making a difference to them, that is when the first foundation for building a great business starts to get created.

The question is, how do you start creating balance? It all starts with working on your emotional balance, found through a feeling of high self-worth, a feeling of joy and fulfilment. It starts when you are able to be happy, even if you have absolutely nothing – yet.

Chapter 2
Find Your Happiness

Believe You Are Worthy

Your self-worth has a lot to do with the actions you take or don't take as an entrepreneur. If you believe you are worthy of achieving a better future, then you are likely to endeavour to get it. If you believe this is not possible, you are likely to be stopped in your tracks and never achieve your full potential.

Tell the Universe and yourself that you are worthy. Appreciate what you have now, and don't focus on what you don't have.

Say affirmations of self-worth to yourself, such as: "I am valuable. I am worthy." Be thankful, and fully appreciate it and feel it as you say the words.
How significant do you feel? Very rarely do we feel significant in the life of an entrepreneur. It's great to feel conscious of what we have achieved and of the decisions we have made to embark on this

journey. As an entrepreneur, you are not always thinking of the immediate return and you may be giving up immediate satisfaction for long-term results.

Look around your network and compare yourself to your peers to understand the choices you have made, and how far ahead or behind you are.

Make others feel significant, as this will reflect back to you in terms of feeling good and a sense of worthiness. Don't look for significance outside of you. Don't feel you are unworthy, even if you don't get significance from others. Know that you aren't getting any significance from others. Don't live your life trying to get any external significance or gratitude from others, because then you are constantly trying, and that's not how it should be. When you expect significance to come from others, you are living in an eternal state of discontentment. Your self-worth is correlated to your happiness.

Do A Happiness Assessment

Whether you are an entrepreneur yet or not, the reality is that you need to first understand where you are so that you can walk in the right direction.

If you don't know where you are, or where you are going, how will you know if you got there?

The path of an entrepreneur starts with identifying your level of happiness. The best way to determine your level of happiness is by taking the time to analyse what makes you feel good.

Feel Good

Feeling good can mean different things to you. It could mean something as small as smiling, or any activity that puts a smile on your face. That can be a physical activity, like walking, running, going to the gym or swimming, or simply meeting your friends, sewing, playing tennis or going to the cinema. Any activity that makes you feel good counts, here: driving, cooking, eating your favourite chocolate, having a massage, mentoring someone.

When you are feeling good, you raise your energy and you become much more attractive to other people, which helps other people connect to you.

Nobody wants to spend time with sad people, especially if they complain.

You become much more attractive to others when you are happy. Your personal happiness acts like a magnet for others. This is because you raise your energy. People are attracted to positive energy and run away from negative energy. Raising your energy, and therefore your magnetism, works for attracting clients, friends, business deals, opportunities and even the right partner – although, of course, in conjunction with the other steps outlined in this book.

Activity:

Ask yourself:

"What makes me feel good?"

Write down at least 100 things that make you feel good here:

Take Care Of Yourself

The next step for believing you are worthy and enhancing your sense of self-worth is to take time to care for your own needs and desires, as well as your body.

When you take the time to groom yourself, have a haircut, have a massage, treat yourself to a nice dinner or something you need, you communicate to the Universe that you are doing things for you because you are worth it. The more well-groomed you are physically, the better you will feel, because you will be looking in the mirror and feeling proud of yourself.

But that alone is not enough. Your real beauty comes from within. When you feel contented with yourself, when you talk to yourself in positive language, and shut down any critical voices that may say you aren't "enough", you create mental peace and happiness, also.

When you take care of yourself spiritually by meditating and taking time to reflect on the answers you need for your business, you are taking care of your soul and energising yourself, as well.

Taking care of yourself energises your mind, body and spirit.

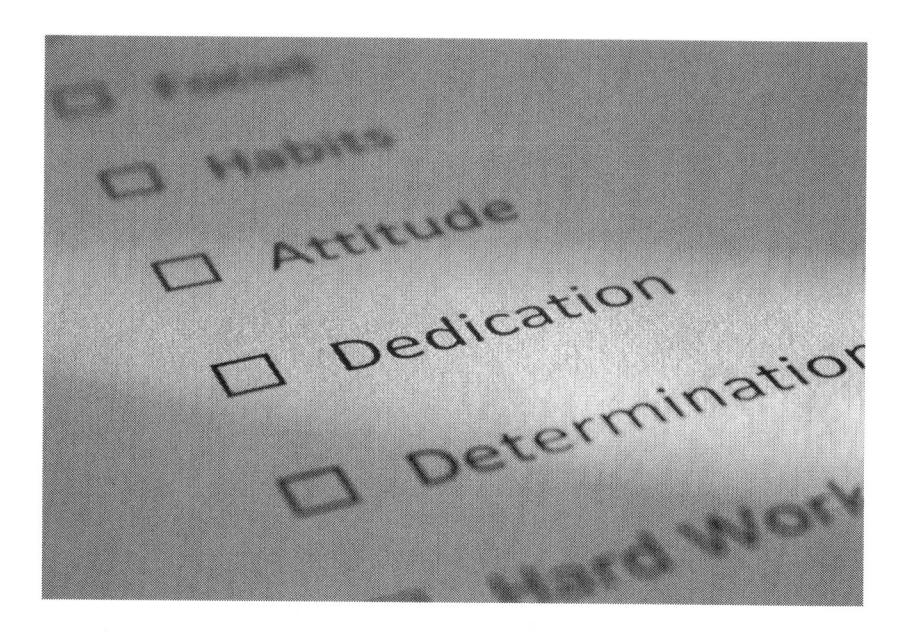

Be Dedicated

Being focused on one thing is very hard for many entrepreneurs, because of the constant need for multitasking.

Being dedicated to one task is very difficult unless you challenge yourself to do this: write everything that needs to be done on index cards or use an online app, such as Asana or Todoist.

They are both fit for creating lists or boards, and allow you to assign tasks to other people to be done.

The best part is that, once you have done them, you can tick off each of these things in asana.com and then the tasks will disappear, which creates less clutter in your diary.

You will also be able to track what you have – or have not – achieved. One good way to focus on one task is to schedule everything in your calendar alongside the dedicated time assigned for it.
Another great way to do it is to write only the task at hand on an index card and work solely on that until you get it done.

The Moment YOU STOP LIVING, YOU START DYING.

Do The Things That You Want To Do

If you are an entrepreneur, you may be doing something you love – if that is the case, then I congratulate you for it. When you love being an entrepreneur, it's great, because you feel you aren't working.

Or, perhaps you may be in a job or business that you hate. If that is the case, then find an aspect or something nice about that particular job and enjoy it fully. Expand that joy to the maximum, even if it is a small part of the day. Even if you hate your job, going out for lunch, meeting your colleagues, or having coffee could be your moment of enjoyment.

If you take this even further and reframe your entire day by thinking about the benefit of working there and feeling contented, no matter what happens at work, you change your perspective, you will raise your energy and you will actually start enjoying your work. Your increased energy will lead to higher productivity, increased engagement with your colleagues, less stress and more happiness.

As a result, you will find it easier to go home and start a side business, if you are an employee currently. It will also become easier to handle work tasks as an entrepreneur.

Another way to do what you really want to do is to find a power team that will complement your skills and enable you to focus on what you are really good at. This alone will increase your energy and magnetism at work, because you will not struggle with tasks you hate or are bad at.

Appreciate What You Have

When you bring gratitude to your life and appreciate every little thing that you are grateful for – then the Universe brings a lot more magnetism and energy to your life. When you are grateful, you are happier. By being positive, you attract more opportunities and clients. You also feel more contented, mentally.

Have A Positive View On Life

When you feel positive, regardless of what happens, you enhance the likelihood of attracting great people, situations, abundance and wealth to you. Nobody feels okay recommending someone who is always complaining.

Add Value To People

If your mindset is focused on collaboration, and on adding value to other people, on serving them and seeing how you can help them, then you attract even more positivity and opportunities to you. You also become more satisfied, knowing you have made a difference.

When you add value to people without expecting anything in return, you create positive energy and positive karma for yourself.

Chapter 3
Find Your Life Purpose

As an entrepreneur, you may see so many opportunities that you feel pulled in different directions – especially in London. If you're like me, you may have experienced "shiny star syndrome" – you're always looking for another opportunity and when you see one, you reach for it.

The question to ask yourself, instead, would be whether you are following a life path that you are proud of and feel privileged to be on.

When you feel proud about what you do, your energy simply shines through. People can feel a great vibe when they are around you, because they feel your passion when you are genuinely enthusiastic about what you do.

The next question to ask yourself is whether what you are doing is in line with what you really want to do.

You will feel happier in your daily routine if what you do is aligned with your life's purpose. You will feel vibrant and excited as you go to work or do any activities because you will be excited about living in general.

Do You Love What You Do?

When you love what you do, you feel energised and become magnetic to others. People start to feel inspired by you. You do work that you love, which is much easier, and faster for you, also.

Odds Are Against You, But You Have To Be

YOUR OWN BET.

If Risk Wasn't An Issue, Would You Still Be Doing The Same Thing?

As entrepreneurs, we often feel trapped in one business. It takes so much time and effort to build a business from the ground up that when we realise our business hasn't worked out, we find it hard to let it go. We stay attached to it, even if it makes losses.

Activity

Think about something that really brings you joy.

Make a list of all the things that bring you joy.

Is there any side business that could be created around your passion?

Write down some potential businesses you could create around your passion.

If you knew that you could not fail, what would you do?

Your Path Finds You

When you are in sync mentally, physically and spiritually, through a combined focus on all these areas, you will find that you will be much more aware of the opportunities that feel right for you. Your purpose will find you. When you find your path, you may not be able to explain it, but it will just simply feel right.

If You Carry On Doing What You Are Doing, Are You Closer To What You Want To Do?

Each thing you do should ideally lead you on a path closer to your ideal business or the life you want to have. There should be a plan, broken down into smaller steps to be taken. These will feel right only if you are aligned from all aspects – mentally, spiritually, physically, emotionally.

Are You Bored?

Your excitement or boredom towards the daily tasks you do each day in your business should be a clue regarding whether you are on the right entrepreneurship path or not.

Chapter 4
Assess How Fulfilled You Are

How fulfilled are you? That should be a question to reflect on. Take a few minutes to yourself, perhaps in the bath, to meditate and think about what you are doing, how things are going and how you can get better.

Take Action In Line With What You Want To Achieve

If you feel like you are not fulfilled, then you may want to take action to put your feet on the path you want to take. You may want to start small, to test out the new path you want to take, and work on your goals little by little. Perhaps you want to try the new path you want to take by volunteering, so you can get an idea of how it really feels before you commit to the new path fully.

If You Are Going To "Chase" Something, CHASE A BETTER VERSION OF YOU.

Work On Yourself

When you are committed to bettering yourself as a person, you realise that it is much easier to operate your business from a higher standard, as well. When you raise your own standards for yourself, it follows quite naturally.

Be "ORIGINAL"
Stop Trying To Copy.

Block Negativity

Complainers, unhappy people and people who feel they can't do anything about their situation are everywhere. It is important to block them out as much as possible, because their energy does affect you, and in the worst possible way. Their energy and their thoughts impact your being negatively, unless you are able to protect yourself from their harmful energy by not being around them.

Be conscious of negative surroundings and go the other way.

Surround Yourself With Positive Environments

When you are in the company of positive, like-minded people, your energy expands. You become more creative and more attractive to others. You start to feel you are in flow. Listen to what others have to say positively about you, since that helps you be yourself, and be happier, also.

Take time for yourself

Spend More Time With Yourself

Spending time alone to reflect is key to discovering solutions for daily business challenges. By doing that, you can tap into your higher consciousness and get the mental clarity needed to take fast business decisions.

Add More Value To Life

When you are focused on adding value to other people, you come across as genuine and helpful. You will find people tend to run away from people who try to sell them stuff. When you focus on helping others and being of service, money will come.

When you are adding value to your environment, you will become more in tune with yourself and your environment. There is a famous saying: energy flows where attention goes.

Connect With Nature

When you connect with nature, your soul gets the chance to disconnect from business pressures and, as a result, when you return to work you will find you are going to be more productive and enjoy your work more. When you don't do that, you become overwhelmed and may not see solutions for your daily business challenges. When you connect with nature, you get the opportunity to make assessments about whether you are fulfilled or not, and listen to the answers from your own mind regarding what is the next move.

Walk in nature. Ground yourself. Walk barefoot in the park, or perhaps in a river or the sea, if you have the opportunity.

Retreat

When you retreat, you give your body, mind and soul a break from the daily distractions and the addiction to your mobile phone or the Internet. This enables you to become much more energised and productive when you are back at work.

I regularly retreat once a year to Peru, in order to spend time with a shaman and to disconnect from the phone and the Internet, and to reconnect with nature and myself. I stay away from distractions and align myself again to what is important.

Do What You Really Want To Do

Focus on doing what you really want to do. Find that business that gives you freedom – whatever freedom means to you – whether it is time, financial and choice freedom. When you choose your business, think about the lifestyle you want to have and picture it. What would it look like?

What adjustments could you make to your work or your business so you can have the lifestyle you want? Get a cleaner, or someone to do small tasks that should be delegated or that you are not good at doing, and focus on those tasks where you are really adding value to the business. This could mean getting a virtual assistant, or getting an intern. You could also do skill swaps or trade one service from your business with another from another business, if you haven't got the money to hire them.

Think about how you can become resourceful in your business. Where can you cut time allocated to certain tasks that don't add value to you? Focus on doing what you want and your productivity will go through the roof.

Ask yourself, "What would I do if money didn't exist?" Try that particular activity on a small scale, so you can experience it and see if you would enjoy it.

Be Conscious Of What Makes You Happy

As entrepreneurs, we need to find a sustainable way of creating and running a business. For that reason, we are always chasing clients, money, opportunities and more. When you shift the focus onto being conscious of what feels rewarding, you start to see change and growth, and you instantly feel great.

By sharing your experience with others, you get instant gratification, because you start feeling comfortable and confident. That, in turn, gives you the belief you can do certain things you didn't use to like doing before.

As an entrepreneur, you may always seek to have confidence in yourself so you can take the right business decisions, but the reality is that confidence will come when you start trying new things. People and situations will seek you out, based on the new things you tried, even if it might not be perfect to start. You will find you will always have something to contribute and you will start to feel comfortable contributing to others.

As an entrepreneur, self-doubt and fear of criticism are big dreams killers. Perhaps you are wondering at times whether you can make it a business or whether your next business venture is going to work. To figure it all out, all you have to do is to believe that you can do it. Risks are necessary, because you never know whether your business is going to be a great success or not. The important thing is to remain balanced, because then, you can cope with anything that may be thrown at you.

Get Inspired

Read about other entrepreneurs or inspirational people who have succeeded, against all odds. Look at the backgrounds of people who have achieved great things, even when starting with nothing. Accept there is no strategy for success. There is no definition for when you are living your purpose, because it's yours and yours only.

Chapter 5
Seek Financial, Time And Choice Freedom

There has to be some sort of feeling of freedom in your life. You will feel freedom when you are doing what you really want to do.

Feeling unrestricted in your choices is important. When you are open-minded and focused on freedom, you see many more possibilities and opportunities for collaboration. When you are stuck doing the same routine tasks and you don't take time to reflect on alternatives, you don't come up with creative ideas and you may find you are feeling trapped in the vicious circle of the same routine.

Don't Worry About What Others Think

The thing that prevents most people from succeeding is the fear of criticism or being judged. I have often fallen prey to this myself, but through reflection and encouraging myself I have managed to push forward and go ahead, in spite of fear.

Create Consistency To Prove Yourself Right

When you are consistently taking actions in line with your goal, you will eventually achieve it. For example, I wanted to become an author and a speaker. Initially, I started by writing down the goal. Then I started writing the notes for the book. Then I took actions to find a publisher. As you can see, the book is done, and it is ready much faster than I initially thought possible, because I took actions consistent with my goal.

I was also dreaming of being a speaker. I was doubting I was ready for it, but I took action, registered on different courses and then, when the opportunity came to speak on stage, I took it. I spoke, and I was astonished by how powerful I was and the impact I had on people.

It is important to feel free to take actions in line with what you want. When you want something but you hold yourself back from taking it, because of self-doubt or fear of criticism, you hold yourself back from success, also.

Achieve A Higher Level Financially

Aim to become financially free, so that you can have the freedom of choice in your life. Whether you are looking to help or contribute to others, or just to live a life where you have the freedom to live on your own terms, when you focus on that you will eventually get it. What you think about, you attract.

Aim To Live A Life Of Options

Focus on creating a life where you have the choice to live as you wish. When you give yourself that challenge, you will attract the opportunities in your life that will enable you to achieve it.

To Change Your Life, You Have To CHANGE Your CHOICES.

Trust Your Gut

Go for it! Even if it doesn't make logical sense, trust your gut feeling. I believe everything that happens in life happens for a reason. When you connect with your desires and dreams by taking time to reflect, or when you simply trust how you feel and you trust the vibe you get about something you are about to do, you will find that you take decisions in line with your goals. When you don't take time to reflect, and you are always rushing or being busy, you are more likely to make mistakes.

Chapter 6
Contribute To The Universe

Can you contribute and add value to life or to people?

When you shift your focus from chasing money to adding value, the energy you put in comes back to you tenfold.

Share Your Expertise

Share the value of what you have to offer with others. When you share your knowledge and expertise, for example, by creating a podcast or a YouTube video to help other people, you will find that the more you give, the more wealth and abundance comes to you.

When you share your experience you will feel a sense of fulfilment. When you freely add value to others, it is a rewarding experience. Get out of your head and share. Don't make a positive or a negative of your ideas or vision. Let others validate what you are thinking and feeling with regard to your adventure and your dream. Do the same for them. Don't look for the let down and the negative in other people. Always approach the positive you can bring out in them.

For example, my business partner said I was a terrible interviewer. He sees things purely from a business perspective, he looks at how this person can perform in a job by identifying their skills and reactions at interview stage, whereas I look at other factors, like attitude, and how motivated the person is. I try to connect with this person's passion and talent to see if they are a good fit for the position available. My last three employees have gone through a very challenging training experience, but have publicly mentioned on other platforms that I am the best boss they have ever worked with. This came from me connecting with them on a deeper level. That was very rewarding for me.

Become A Business Coach

Put yourself in a position where you can provide advice to others on a business or personal level. Put yourself in a place where you have the financial and time freedom to do it, because the best way to add value to others and learn something yourself is by teaching something to someone else.

Be Emotionally Intelligent

When you connect with others and you are fully present as you speak to them, you will find that you are getting more out of the same conversation because you are listening properly, as opposed to just waiting for your turn to speak.

Connect With Yourself

Become more self-aware. When you become more aware of your feelings and you focus on connecting with yourself more, you will be able to connect with others, also. When you love yourself fully and profoundly, you will be able to love others, also, and because of that they will feel it and they will be attracted to you, giving you more business opportunities.

You create in the world what you are or what you say to yourself you are. When you say to yourself "I am LOVE," you express that in the world in terms of actions, and the world responds to you. You become more authentic, and more accepting of who you really are, with all your weaknesses and strengths.

It Is Not Your Past That Dictates Who You Will Become, It Is Your Present "YOU" Who Decides.

Read The Universal Signs

It doesn't matter whether you are religious or not. This has nothing to do with religion, but with accepting that the Universe always sends you signs that you may decide to follow or not. The Universe collaborates with you and helps you in your journey. You can use this strategy in your business, simply by becoming more aware of what is happening around you, what signals the Universe is sending you through the things that occur, the people you meet, the events that happen, and the messages or the signs that you see written around you.

Chapter 7
Be Aware Of Potential Improvement

Is it possible you could be doing better in any area of your life? If the answer is yes, here is what you could do:

Identify Your Weaknesses

Become aware of what you hate doing or simply struggle with. You can choose to either master your weaknesses and become great at those particular activities you typically hate or you can choose to delegate them to other people, who can complete those tasks better and faster.

Be Conscious Of What You Could Be Doing Better And More Of

When you identify areas you could improve on and you take action consistent with your goal, you become unstoppable, because doors start to open as a result of it. When you become more, you receive more.

Learn New Skills

Improving yourself by learning new skills makes you grow as a person and also enhances the possibilities and opportunities available to you.

Enhance Your Existing Skills

It takes ten thousand hours to become a master at something. When you do something for an extensive period of time, you become better every time you do it. Spend time enhancing your skills and you will discover a whole new world will open for you. The top 1% wealthiest and most abundant people on Earth are typically those who continuously strive to improve, innovate and implement their ideas faster and more efficiently.

Don't Settle For Who You Are

It is important that you have a commitment to continuous improvement. When you continuously keep going forward, by discovering and applying the latest cutting edge techniques in your field, you will be able to become the leader in your area of expertise and monetise your knowledge better, also.

Exercise

Exercise will relieve blockage, which will enhance your abilities and strengths, allowing you to take on new challenges. It will also give you the energy and boldness to keep going forward, despite any obstacle you may encounter in your business.

Improve Your Productivity

Why is it that billionaires and other successful people have the same 24 hours in a day as everyone else, but are able to do so much more with their time?

It is because they have mastered the art of high productivity. The question is, how can you achieve the same thing? Here is what I have discovered and that has helped me:

Write Down Your Daily Structure

In order to become more effective in terms of using your time, you need to understand how much time you are putting in to different areas of your life. You can analyse this easily, by writing down how much of your time is spent doing different things during the course of the day. Record it in terms of blocks of time.

Try to understand how much reward you are getting from the time you are putting in, and what areas you get the most reward from. Once you have analysed this, aim to minimise the time you spend on certain activities in order to give more time to other areas that aren't performing as well.

Value Your Time

You need to be aware of how valuable your time is and be very strict with how you spend it. Your time may be better spent in activities such as sales, business development or marketing, and less well spent in areas such as customer service, cleaning the house or ironing.

Balance All Areas Of Your Life

Use, for example, a chart system in order to measure how you are doing in all areas of your life. Assign each chart column to an area of your life. You can include different colours to symbolise different aspects of your life: your physical, emotional, spiritual, and financial well-being, the time spent on family, relationships and work. If you look at the chart, the columns should be more or less even. This should give you clarity on the areas that need attention. The same amount of energy needs to be given to all areas.

Monitor Your Well-being, Weekly And Daily

Monitor your activities daily – or at least weekly – so that you can keep track of what is not working and so make any necessary adjustments.

Buy Time

Time is the most valuable resource, because it cannot be replaced. If you can get a coach who can shortcut your way to success, you should totally get it, because a coach can buy you time so that you don't need to struggle.

Buy Structures Or Systems

Know your worth to understand certain areas of your life need the same amount of energy.

If you are running a successful business, you may find it worthwhile to buy systems and tools that can enable you to do your work more efficiently. It all comes back to return on investment. If you can invest in a system that will save you or make you an extra 25% per month or per year, then over five years, how much is that worth to you?

Build New Relationships Daily

If you focus on building relationships rather than on chasing money, the money will come to you.

You can build great relationships by giving first. Instead of thinking about what you can sell to this person, think about how you can serve or help this person to achieve their goals. You are then going to be in a better position to attract more clients and more sales. When you come from a place of serving and helping others, they can feel your energy and they feel attracted to doing business with you or referring others to you.

Just Know You Can Always Do More

The reality is that you have unlimited potential. When you fully embrace that, and you take steps to unleash that full potential, you will realise there is so much more you can achieve. What is that one step or tiny difference in the way you run your business that will help you achieve more than you expect?

For example, by hiring a virtual assistant who can take calls for your company or can do some admin work, you can relieve yourself of some time spent on unnecessary activities, and can leverage that time better in another activity that brings you better returns.

Position Yourself To Perform

When you prepare your body for success, everything is easier. You can do this by having an active lifestyle or by exercising.

The body has to release some energy. You can stretch or walk or do any exercise you like. This doesn't just help make your body stronger, fitter and more supple, it can help with depression and anxiety, too. You can take long walks in nature or socialise with like-minded people. When you do that, your energy raises and you are able to perform better. You are able to also bounce ideas off others and come up with better ways of doing the same thing.

You also need time alone. You don't need to be a hermit, but do take time to meditate, so that you feel energised when you are at work. When you are not thinking negative thoughts you are in flow and you are able to perform better. Reward yourself with holidays, because it is during times where you are able to fully switch off that your best ideas come to life.

Be Conscious Of Your Nutrition

When you feed well, you get much more energy and enthusiasm at work. Avoid coffee and dairy products and, instead, focus on eating a balanced alkaline diet, where fruits and vegetables are prevalent. Focus on eating better and drinking more water. Lack of water makes you dehydrated, which makes it difficult for you to focus at work, because your brain needs the water to function properly.

Invest In Yourself

Warren Buffett, one of the world's richest billionaires, talks about the fact that the best investment you can make is in yourself.

Invest time in improving yourself, whatever that means to you.

Invest in learning from different training courses or books, and focus on continuous improvement, because the more you know and understand about the world and the area your business operates in, the more prepared you are for taking better business decisions.

Take Time To Know And Understand Yourself

Take Time To Be Alone

Taking time to reflect, by yourself, will give you creative ideas and bring clarity to your life. As an entrepreneur, it is very hard to take any time to yourself because it feels you could be doing so much, instead, but that reflection time is required so that you can get into a state of flow and produce so much more during your time at work.

Ask Yourself Questions

Question yourself and write down how you feel about different things. That will liberate your mind and enable you to become more creative and more resourceful at work.

Watch Inspirational Videos

When you watch inspirational videos, for example, videos of Sadhguru that are in line with the feeling you are trying to exude, you are going to start to feel in flow.

Explore Healing Methods

When you are open to the idea of healing yourself, you are able to become a lot more productive. You can heal yourself with spiritual practices or even through meditation.

Understand Energy

You may not be aware, but the energy of the people around you – whether that is negative or positive – directly impacts you. People's thoughts impact you, also. Imagine going on the Tube and being impacted by every person's thoughts! Instead, if your energy is high and you use certain spiritual practices in order to protect your energy and in order to prevent the negative energy from affecting you, you will find that you attract more of what you want into your life.

There are some spiritual practices that you can do at home in only ten minutes in order to shift your negative energy and bring more positive energy.

Everything in the Universe is energy. When you understand that, you will realise that the more energy you put into something, the more energy you attract to you.

Push away negative thoughts. Move your body every time you feel negative so that you can change your state and start thinking positively.

Whilst thinking negatively, no good things, opportunities or situations will be attracted to you. If they are, you will find a way to repel them with your negative energy.

Do your best to be kind to everyone, since your environment is a mirror of yourself. You attract more of what you are. Motivational speaker, Les Brown, says:

"You don't get in life what you want, you get in life what you are."

Your results are going to be a mirror of your actions. Be considerate and approach other businesses from a collaborative perspective, rather than focusing on denigrating the competition. When you send negative energy into the Universe, you get more of it back.

You need to find a way to use the energy of the Universe and not go against it, by only focusing on positivity and collaboration.

When you apply consistency to meditation by doing it every day you will start to feel more at peace with yourself and your energy will raise.

Aim To Be Comfortable In Your Own Self

The main thing that holds back many entrepreneurs is negative self-talk. The voice in your head keeps asking, *What if it won't be good enough? What if you fail?* That critical inner voice is just trying to keep you safe in your comfort zone, but the fact is that you can only grow if you expand your comfort zone, and you can only do that if you are comfortable with who you are.

Know that your potential really is limitless, and all you need to do is to believe in yourself.

Take Deep Breaths Throughout The Day

Most people don't know how important it is to oxygenate our brain and breathe properly. When you bring oxygen to your brain, you can be clearer about the tasks at work and perform much better. Your breathing brings a moment of "now" – which is very important.

Be Fully Present

Aim to be present, regardless of what you are doing. When you give 100% attention to your current moment, you get more out of it. When you are 100% present with your friends, family or co-workers, they feel important and they also feel listened to. Your solutions for your business or life challenges are always within you or around you. When you are fully present, you are able to connect more with those around you and at a deeper level.

Aim To Feel More And Think Less

Make more decisions based on feeling rather than thinking, especially when it's something regarding you, rather than a situation. Trust your gut feeling. When you rely more on how you feel rather than on what makes sense at first sight, you will make better judgements because you will allow your intuition to help you in your decisions. I have learnt to trust the process and believe things will work out just fine, despite not always looking that way at first sight.

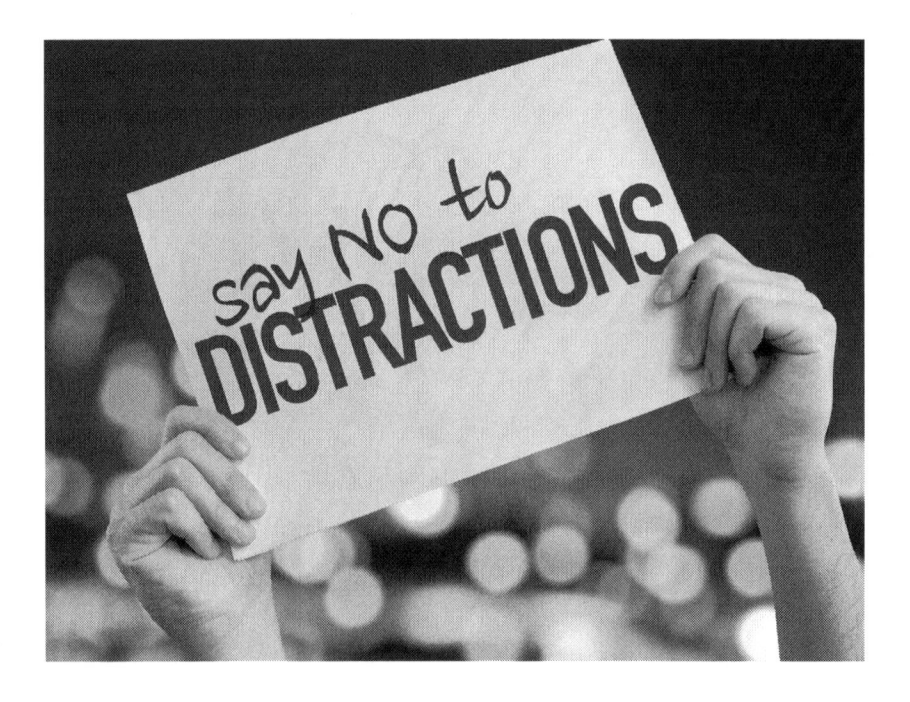

Lessen Distractions

Identify what you are dedicating time to and avoid distractions from matters that aren't contributing to that topic. Learn to control temptation by starting with the little tasks, first. Know who distracts you and start building your network to avoid further distractions. Allow extra time for the odd distraction that is important. Prepare your schedule to include, for example, a bit of time in between meetings to allow for unexpected things that may occur.

Control Your Thoughts

Focus on what is to be done with the help of classical music, the right nutrition and by getting back to the task in hand any time you get sidetracked. You can "bribe" yourself with a little treat for finishing a task.

Be Disciplined

Be disciplined to do things in line with your growth. You will find that the more you grow as a person, the easier it gets to handle bigger and bigger projects that would have seemed insurmountable not so long ago.

Break Through Your Blockages

You need to go through the blockages you have built as a result of past conditioning and what people said you are. You identified the person you think you are a long time ago. Every day, you are acting in accordance with the person you think you are, without realising that every single day, you grow as a person and become much better. You are pretending you are still the same person you were when you were younger, which keeps you taking small actions. You might think, *I am a selfish person*, and the Universe or the people around you might tell you that's not who you are, which will bring you one step closer to breaking down that system which isn't you.

As you are getting new challenges, you are proving to yourself and the Universe that you are able to grow, by overcoming adversity and obstacles.

Chapter 8
The More You Fail, The Closer You Are To Success

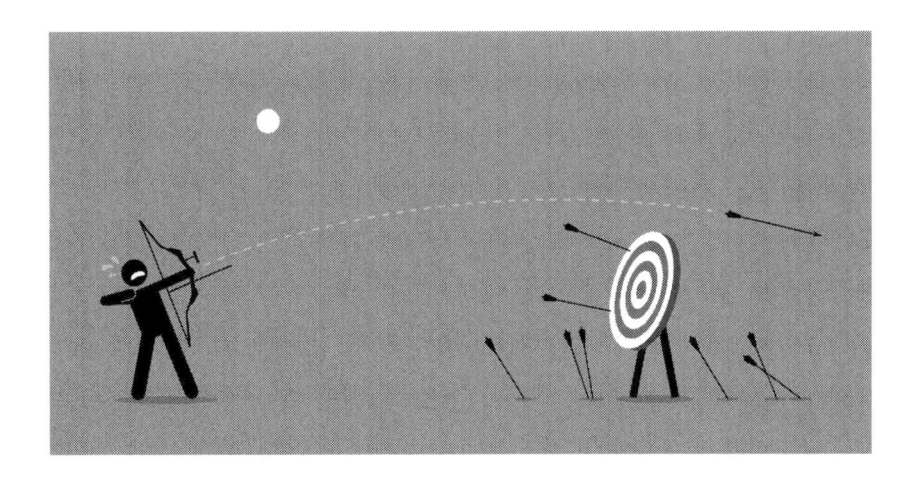

Failure Is An Inherent Part Of Succeeding

As an entrepreneur, you need to come to terms with failure. On your journey to success, there will be a lot of things that may not work, but that is because there are other paths you are supposed to take. You will meet people who both challenge you and support you – both have a role in your life, and that is to lead you on the right path in order to achieve progress and fulfil your unlimited potential.

Fear of failure as an entrepreneur can lead to "paralysis by analysis". Have you ever been at a point in your life where you are at a crossroads in business and you simply don't know which way to go? Have you ever experienced that moment – or perhaps days, months, even years – where you have thought about taking a certain course of action and you simply could not decide, despite knowing in your heart it was the right thing to do?

The fear of failure could prevent you from taking any decision and instead, keep you where you are. It takes courage to make a powerful decision to go after your dreams as an entrepreneur.

It takes courage to keep going in spite of knowing you may not get business, or you may be criticised. It takes a really big heart and a lot more courage than many people are able to muster.

Failure needs to be accepted – it is a part of the process – but the key thing is to accept that despite failing many times, you have got to trust the process and know in your heart that you will find a way to succeed.

Whilst you are striving to succeed, sacrifices may have to be made. Be ready to disconnect with friends and family or relationships; be ready to potentially go bankrupt. Be ready to lose yourself. Be ready to live many years in a dark place. Be ready to walk alone or be ashamed. Be ready to struggle with self-worth.

There may be points on your entrepreneurship journey where you feel like the weight of the world is on your shoulders and you are feeling lost.

All odds may appear to be against you, and you must be ready to not achieve whatever it is you embarked upon to achieve. You may feel you are wasting your time, you may not know what to do or which direction to go. You may harm yourself in many ways, not just physically. You may question yourself constantly, but the reality is that the Universe has a much greater plan for you than you ever imagined. When you have reached your lowest level of desperation, the important thing is not to give up, because growth is on the other side of hardship and endurance. Opportunities will flourish and will start to manifest into your life if you start working on yourself, physically, emotionally, spiritually.

When you embark on a journey of discovery in order to align all these key areas, that is when you will experience everything you desire and much more will start manifesting in your life.

FAILURE
Is A Sign You Are Moving Forward.

You need to be ready to fail. Accept that failure is part of the journey. You need to believe, trust the process, have patience and keep moving or showing up. It is only when you show up to your commitments that the Universe repays you with the right opportunities, wealth and abundance you desire.

Focus On The Achievement, Not On The Failure

As you are going through failures, the hardest thing is to stay motivated. The best way to do it is to constantly visualise your dream, regardless of the reality today. Absorb each failure as being one step closer to achieving it and stay positive by thinking about what you are going to accomplish in the future.

FEEL
The Journey To Success And
MASTER
The Thinking Of Failure.

Plan For Success, But Expect To Fail

Your journey to success will incur a lot of failure, disappointment and pain. The bigger your goal, the longer the time frame it may take to achieve it. Be prepared to have failure on the way to success, but take consistent action in order to succeed.

You need to understand that failure happens before success does. Remember that this journey of success as an entrepreneur is new territory and you have never walked this road before.

Expand Your Comfort Zone

Position yourself out of your comfort zone all the time. You need to explore new territory, new ways of acting in your entrepreneurial journey and accept that everyone fails before they succeed. Accept it and keep planning the road ahead. You need to have a strong vision of the person you will become at the end of the journey.

It Will Question You, Break You, Build You And "Make You"
A SUCCESS.

Accept You May Need To Sacrifice

What price are you willing to pay to achieve a better you? There is no such thing as something for nothing. Sacrifices have to be made in order to get access to your higher consciousness and a bigger you. Whether that is sacrificing time with your family, time for fun or anything else, remember that sacrifices always have consequences. A lot of sacrifice or a feeling of unfulfillment can lead someone to suicide.

When you are balanced spiritually, you don't get to that place, despite any failures or obstacles you may encounter. I used to be very unbalanced. Then

I started following spiritual practices that enabled me to find more clarity and made my thoughts more visual.

Even though at that point you can't see it, you believe one day you will achieve what you desire by continuously working on your inner self. If you practice meditation, you will notice it alleviates the suffering and makes the process a bigger light at the end of the tunnel. Acknowledge you might write a book about it when your suffering is over.

Be Strict With Your Time

Time is limited. Be conscious of what you are giving time to. You don't have much, so when you are doing any activity, give it your undivided attention. When you are working on too many projects, it is difficult for the Universe to help you. Focus your attention on your dream. Don't divide yourself in too many directions and do be selective about who or what you are giving your time to. Focus on doing more and talking less. Dedicate time to improving yourself, because you can't help others until you have helped yourself, first. You have to fill your own cup before you share with others. On the plane, you will notice the cabin crew always mention you should put your own oxygen mask on first, then help others. It is the same concept. Pay attention to you. You should be the number one priority, so that you will have the physical and emotional strength to deal with heartache, failure and pain.

You May Need To Sacrifice Time With Family Or Friends

As you are working on your dreams, you may need to temporarily stay away from your friends, family, relationships, or the hobbies you love.

You may need to say no to challenges or battles that aren't worth your time. You may need to say no to things that are not furthering your dreams. Just know in those darkest moments of desperation that there is a light at the end of the tunnel.

You May Have To Face Bankruptcy

You may go through not having money, not being able to get credit, or you may go through a period where you are feeling stuck. You may end up in a situation where nobody wants to work with you. At times, you may feel like a real failure. You may consider becoming a hermit and may have limited options to move forward. Embracing and believing all that we know and hear about bankruptcy becomes a belief. You may feel like you really have no idea what to do because there seems to be no way out. When you are in that place of desperation, you need to know that there is always a way to get out. The solution is within. When you work on balancing yourself, you start manifesting your desires.

You May Have To Face A Lack Of Fun

As you are going through dry months, with not enough income to pay the staff or your expenses, you may have to say no to parties because you feel unworthy. Perhaps you may even feel you haven't achieved enough to be there or you are not good enough to attend. You may feel you are struggling because you are perceived as anti-social, and there is no entertainment. You need to sacrifice in the short term for long-term achievements. That is what it takes to become a highly successful entrepreneur.

Build Relationships

The relationships that I built during my journey as an entrepreneur helped me turn everything around, just as I was feeling really hopeless. It's not something that can be explained.

I want to share the belief, processes and self-conditioning you need to have to endure the process. You may struggle with the endurance of the process.

The entrepreneur paradox is that when you focus on chasing money, the faster the money runs away from you. When you focus on growing as a person, you are going to achieve your dream goal through organic growth.

When You Feel Life Is Beating You Down,

BELIEVE

That You Are Right Where You're Supposed To Be.

You May Have To Deal With Shame

When you are an entrepreneur, you are so focused on dealing with your dream that you don't deal with shame. In 2012, I just wanted someone to put a hand on my shoulder and say, "Sandro, failure is part of the process."

I didn't understand that and so I had no awareness of what would happen. I didn't understand failure was part of the process. That is why psychology happens better in groups. If we don't share the blueprint, then people won't know how to do things.

How I managed to tackle it was by absorbing the situation, the shame, all those energies I was feeling, and identify they were there. I positioned myself in the future, rather than in the current reality, mentally.

I had to be positive. I had to hope each day was going to bring me one step closer to my dream. This was the reason I was so driven.

As you are working on your hopes and aspirations, you can't let go of that dream because, if you do, the current reality will take over.

If you focus a lot of energy on all those things you want to achieve, you are going to achieve them, because the focus is always on the dream and knowing you are worthy of it.

By the time these topics of sacrifice and failure start coming in at this level, you are at breaking point, and things can go one of two ways – either self destruction or seeing the light at the end of the tunnel. As you are dealing with failure, you could feel like you are starting to lose yourself; you may face public humiliation, endure constant battles within, struggle with trying to take the right decisions, and suffer from lack of sleep.

When you change your strategy and you focus on creating an amazing you, you will <u>create</u> a product or a service that is delivered just right. Everything you launch becomes amazing because your energy is focused on creating greatness rather than on making money.

Make An Impact On The World

Is your desired goal or achievement bigger than you?

Your dreams need to have an impact on more people than just you. It's not about what your desired achievement does for you, it's about what you can do with it for humanity.

Create and follow a dream that would make an impact and a difference, because then, the Universe will help you achieve it. Ask yourself what it will do for others, besides giving you the satisfaction of achieving it.

Is everything you are looking to step into bigger than you? It's not just about you; it's about impact. People are going to form a good impression of you because you know you're going to have a much bigger impact than just on you. Everything you do impacts on what's around you.

I started succeeding when I realised what I was doing had to have a greater impact on the world, not just on me. Have some substance to this entrepreneurial journey. Focus on creating an impact on the world. It all starts with you. Don't chase money, fame, significance.

Create Something That Makes A Difference

If you create a hospital, create it not because you want to be rich. Create it because you want to contribute and help people. If it's just for your own pride or use, you won't achieve your goals as easily, as you are chasing money. The moment your achievement has an impact on other people is when you will find you succeed.

People say, "I want 30k, 40k." They are always chasing money. When you decide to go on a journey of growth, but the result you want to achieve isn't bigger than you, you will be forever chasing. Have a core substance to your dream that you always act from. That is when the Universe will conspire to help you achieve your goals.

Get The Validation That You Are Adding Value Or Making A Difference

As you are building your business, don't focus on making money. Keep going and focus on the value being added and the difference made in the world. Concentrate on occupying territory or presence in the marketplace before making money a priority, because that will enable you to attract influencers, collaborators and joint venture partners with similar views on the world. You will then have a much bigger force and motivation as a uniting element, which will enable you to prosper in your business faster than if you were to simply focus on making money.

A JOURNEY

To Live, Not To Chase, Find You, Before You Find Success.

Chapter 9
Identify Your Talents

Your Talent Finds You

I strongly believe that when you work on yourself mentally, physically, spiritually, you attract your talent to you.
Your talent is so common sense to you that perhaps when you are imbalanced you don't even notice it. Your talent is something that feels so natural and easy for you to do and yet it may be so hard for

other people. Many entrepreneurs have managed to monetise their talents – even something as simple as their passion for travelling, speaking, asking great questions, dancing.

Identify what you are good at. You will know you are good at it when you ask yourself and other people: "What am I really good at?"

Then listen to the answers. The more common sense it feels, the better you are at it. What is that one thing that fills you up with joy, instantly, when you do it? What is that one thing that makes you feel excited and vibrant when you do it?

Working on your inner self is a contribution to the space you need internally to identify your true talent. You need to go through different processes of life to identify what's enjoyable and natural to you.

Surround Yourself With Positivity

When you are in an environment that is vibrating at a high frequency, you may not know why, but you simply feel good. You become more productive and you feel in flow. The same work that took you hours to do or the calls that you struggled to make are now achieved in a fraction of the time, because you feel in flow and are in your peak state.

This is because the energy of the people around us impacts us positively – and negatively, too. If you are in a conference room where people previously argued, the energy just doesn't feel right. When you surround yourself with positivity, you attract greater opportunities and influencers to you, and everything seems to click into place, as if it were a piece of a puzzle.

Be On A Mission To Find Yourself

You need to continuously be on a mission to find and express your true authentic self to the world. When you do that, your entire being exudes confidence, as you start attracting to you those exact people who need you, and who you need.

Ride The Darkness, Lose Yourself And You Will **FIND YOURSELF.**

Start finding out what others like about you or feel that you are good at. Write down these things.

What others perceive as very obvious about your talent may not be obvious to you. When you listen, not only to yourself but also to what people say you are good at, you may realise unexpected talents you didn't know you had.

Improve a particular skill that you are conscious of or believe could be your talent. Whilst you may have an ability for learning quickly or for a particular skill, there are other abilities that can be developed by spending hours mastering these skills. Every master was once a disaster, as they say. It takes ten thousand hours to become great at a particular skill, so if you feel you are not particularly gifted, you can develop certain skills through practice.

Network With Others

Be open-minded as you network with others and start having conversations about your talent. Do as much as possible so you can reach a wider audience – whether that is through social media, networking events or anywhere you are able to impact as many people as possible.

Try to see others' validation regarding your talent as more valuable and worthy than your own validation regarding your talent. Be patient, and don't force it to be a life path too early. Allow your path in life to form and build. Trust that the validation you need regarding your talent will be as clear as light when the time is right.

Be Persistent In Working On Yourself

The entrepreneur paradox is that no matter how hard you try, if you don't feel good – mentally, physically and spiritually – every execution in the physical world will not have a positive outcome. We can't achieve our dream or success level, being who we are. We need to grow ourselves in all areas to become or achieve what we want. When we understand the mind needs to change and we, as people, need to change, internally and externally, we will make it a priority to be persistent with our own internal growth.

You need to know that working on you will create a better you. As you create a better you, everything that you execute in the physical world will be positive.

Make yourself the number one priority by applying consistency to being active, to stillness, and to taking action to focus on bringing your talent to light.

Chapter 10
How To Build On Your Belief

Just Do It

Regardless of the business you are in, you need to take consistent action towards your goals, in spite of fear. You need to look at how can you best utilise the resources in your business, the skills you have, the tools and strategies you have, in order to achieve a desired result. If you haven't got certain resources, you need to ask yourself: "How can I become more resourceful?" "How can I leverage what I have and my network so that I can achieve the outcome I am expecting?"

When you have a task to do, just get it done.

Don't talk yourself out of doing it with negative self-talk. When you do something, you have the opportunity to get it done better next time. When you put yourself down by thinking it is not good enough, you may end up not doing it at all, which is much worse.

As you start doing something new, it is frustrating to see how it is not perfect. In fact, it may take a long time before it is perfect. But have you seen any baby who comes out of the womb and starts walking perfectly? Surely, you have not. It is the same thing. Unless you get it done one time, you can't get it done better. The first few times it may not be the way you would like it to be, but as long as you keep going, you will end up getting to the right result.

Get Creative And Resourceful

If you are investing in or developing property, as I am, you may consider looking at financial options, if you haven't got the investment money yourself.

The important part is to create a power team around you that will enable you to take your business to the next level. This may mean partnering up with people to complement your skills or resources. You may consider doing a skill swap or a trade of your services.

If you are in property, for example, you could consider forming a partnership in which one person spends their time managing the project, another puts in the investment, but doesn't have any time to spend working on the project, another gets the mortgage, and another deals with getting the planning approved by the local council, or whoever is in charge of granting approvals for planning. How you do it depends on what you want to do.

Activity

Ask yourself: "How can I become resourceful or creative in my business?"

Write down a few ways you could become resourceful or creative in your business, so you can save money.
Write down what you would do differently.

Write down a few ways you could become resourceful or creative in your business, so you can make more money or get more clients.
Write down what you would do differently.

Write down a few ways you could become resourceful or creative in your business so you can save time.
Write down what you would do differently.

Write down a few ways you could become resourceful or creative in your business so you can do more of what you love, and less of what drags you down or that you feel out of flow with.
Write down what you would do differently.

You will discover that, when you surround yourself with people who relate to your dream or goal, you will learn key things from others and they will also learn from you. Share what you want to do with positive people, because their support – even if it is just emotional support – will help you go further in your business endeavours.

Believe You Can Do It

You will get multiple windows of opportunity to share your talent with the world. You need to be open-minded, to actively search out these opportunities, and be proactive and say yes when they appear. This is likely to happen if you believe, deep in your heart, that you can do it. Belief in yourself may not come naturally to you. It's a process that starts with taking small steps in the right direction.

Take advantage of every little window of opportunity to share your talent with others. Doing this is something of a catch-22 situation, because it can be daunting, and yet until you do it, you won't get the validation of your talent from anyone. The more you share your talent, the more confidence you build as you get good at it and you also get acknowledged for it by others. If you are like thousands of other people and you are always wondering whether you are good enough, you simply need to allow your talent to unfold and play down your little voice – your negative self-talk, which is trying to keep you small and that interferes with your belief that you are worthy.

Find Every Opportunity To Share Your Talent

Put yourself in situations where you can express what you are trying to do. For example, I had a dream that someday I would become a speaker and I actively searched for speaking opportunities. When the chance arose, I put myself forward for speaking, despite not feeling prepared.

Identify Those Who Are Doing Something Similar

It is important to identify those people who seem to be doing the exact thing you want to be doing, so that you can learn from them. Take time to understand what they are doing, then identify key areas you like, so that you can model them. You can also identify areas you feel could be improved on or done differently.

Be ready to work with people who are already doing what you want to do in order to collaborate with them and learn from them, so you don't need to struggle to learn the ropes.

Understand How You Will Be Different

As well as analysing people who are running a similar business to the one you are running or intend to run, remember that there could be a lot to be learnt from others that have been in the same business for a long time. You need to analyse what is working well in their businesses and determine what differentiation or unique selling point you are going to create in your business; it should be something that is likely to work better in your business. You have got to believe that your differentiation is the reason why your business will work better.

CREATE THE OPPORTUNITY,
Do Not Wait For One To Come.

Don't Put Too Much Pressure On Yourself

Building your business requires time. You need to understand that and trust the process. Focus on making more noise about your business and attracting more exposure and awareness for what you are offering. Don't set a timeline for the result or the success of your vision. Instead, invest time into you and your talent. Don't compare yourself to others based on their achievements and the time it has taken them. Trust what you desire will happen for you, providing you are consistent in your actions.

Let Your Talent Blossom

Believe in the intention you put out in the world and trust the outcome. Focus on feeling fulfilled, knowing that you are living a life true to yourself and others.

Start Small, Build Big

The hardest step you take in your business is the first one. Whether that is making a change that will ultimately lead to a huge difference, as an entrepreneur you are always taking risks. Some of them lead to great abundance and some lead to huge losses. The key thing is to take multiple small steps, and keep adjusting your direction until it feels right.

One really important step in the life of an entrepreneur is to improve continuously, because a momentum of small steps will give you the confidence to take a big momentum of steps.

Chapter 11
How To Stay Consistent

Visualise Your Outcome

Visualise what you are working for and see clearly your end result, regardless of your current reality. Do affirmations regarding who you are, in the present tense and related to things you want to manifest in your life. Feel yourself achieving and talk about yourself achieving. Engage all your senses in the visualisation. Feel, see, touch, smell the items in your desired reality as if it were there with you now.

The picture of your end goal needs to be in the future, making this your reality.

Ask yourself whether your business is worth your effort in the long run. What will you be able to do once you achieve what you want? How would you live? Who would you help? How significant will you feel? How much power will you have? Do you deserve this? Why would it not be possible? How many relationships and networks will you build? How much self-worth will you have? How much time can you buy? How would you experience life from that point?

Make Decisions In Line With Where You Want To Go

Make decisions based on what you want to achieve and based on the path you want to go down. Don't spread your decisions throughout your day. Block out time for deciding important decisions and leave small decisions to others.

Show Up Consistently And Do Something Towards Your Goal

Don't lose faith in your entrepreneurial vision. Do show up and perform at work to the best of your ability. Baby steps are fine. On bad days, making no step towards your goal is fine, but at least show up and try doing a little more than yesterday. Aim for a specific result.

Identify Why You Are Doing It

Remind yourself daily why you are doing this, because your motivation or lack of drive derives from a strong or weak reason why. Visualise the achievement and feel the impact it will have on others. You could be inspiring someone without knowing.

If You Can Feel It,
YOU CAN ACHIEVE IT,

If You Can Think It,
YOU CAN MATERIALISE IT.

Start With The End In Mind

Never lose focus of the desired success or the dream you have in your mind. Regardless of what's being done now, focus on your vision. Learn to set your mind on the vision and you will find yourself very driven and motivated, especially when it involves other people, not yourself. You will find you will do much more for your children, your parents or your spouse than for yourself. You will also find that money may not motivate you as much as a desire to contribute to a cause.

Stay Focused On Your Dream

During your times of failure and pain, visualisation is a great tool to help you stay focused on your goal in tough times. You can tap into this at any time, as it is a great tool to fuel you.

Your reason "why" and the visualisation removes you from the current reality and enables you to cope with difficult times.

YOUR DREAM
Will Drive You,

FAILURE
Will Break You,

BALANCE
Will Make You A Success.

Chapter 12
How To Achieve Physical Balance

Maintain An Active Lifestyle

Whilst running your business, you absorb a lot of energy from the people around you – whether that is your clients, neighbours, work colleagues, even people you are travelling on the bus with.

That negative energy that gets accumulated needs to be cleansed, so that you are able to manifest abundance and become magnetic to everything you desire. This negative energy that gets piled up isn't something you should be working with. You need an active lifestyle in order to release this negative energy through sweat. Take your mind off things that didn't work in your business and get a massage. Releasing excess energy is super-important if you are to have a balanced entrepreneur lifestyle, because you carry so much weight and so much pressure, daily.

This release of excess energy through physical exercise is required so you can "empty your cup" and allow flow to occur. Your energy is not flowing if you aren't releasing this negative energy and if you don't have an active lifestyle. It's the first step that enables you to take control, take action, and start to be consistent. It builds control and discipline and you will start to see a difference in your results. You can release excess energy through walks, gym, massage, boxing or any sort of physical exercise – but not through something relaxing.

Stick To A Routine:

I exercise six days a week – mornings are better, because you never know what time your day will end, but you can plan what time you start. You can start with you. There is no excuse if you aren't a morning person. There is no excuse why anyone should not be working on them. That is a limiting belief, if you believe you can't do it because xyz reason.

If you take the challenge of exercising in the morning you will be able to get close to miraculous results: release overloaded information in your mind, and release overloaded weight in your physical body. You will be able to unblock unnecessary energy blockages, stay focused, release stress, work for a better version of you, feel happy because your body releases dopamine, which enables you to feel the sensation of happiness.

You will also be able to balance reaction time with action time at work. Have you ever noticed how sometimes you are just reacting to situations at work, rather than being proactive? Well, by exercising first thing in the morning you will become much more proactive and more calm, and less snappy and reactive when something happens at work.

Exercise will also enable you to balance your lifestyle between the intensity at work and the necessity to work on you. It will also enable you to have peace with yourself and give you a sense of achievement. Your mind will feel clearer, more focused on productivity and structure. You will also be better equipped for overcoming challenges.

If you want to commit to taking the exercise challenge for 30 days, follow me on Instagram and tag me with the hashtag #30daychallenge at @keeping_up_with_trio. As you know, challenges taken as a group are more effective, as you feel more accountable when you declare your intent publicly.

Where To Exercise

The easiest possible solution is to undertake your exercise activity as close to your home or your work as possible. The further away it is, in terms of distance and travelling time, the harder it is to stick to your routine. You are the entrepreneur and you can decide where you spend your time.

Achieving physical balance needs to be worked on if you want to be a healthy "athlete of life". People see the result of an athlete at the gym. For us entrepreneurs to be successful there are forms of discipline and consistency that will enable us to perform at peak performance. I call it "athlete of life" because, as an entrepreneur, unless you reach mastery in all these areas, you will not be able to succeed long term. You will find that you built a business, but neglected your spouse. Or you built a business but you had a heart attack because you didn't feed well for an extensive period of time.

You can't be great at making money and put time and energy at everything you do. You never can sacrifice yourself. You need an element of balance. Certain areas will be given more energy, of course. If you spend 8 hours on entrepreneurship but don't do 30 minutes on YOU, you fail. It's as important to work on you as it is to work on your business.

Connection with nature and running in the park will, of course, be preferable when you are exercising, but in the absence of it, other ways of exercising are okay – the gym or yoga centres, for example. It is important to hang out with a network of like-minded friends. You can find advice on how to eat in a balanced way through online nutrition advice or online personal trainers.

<u>Trust and know</u> it's important to do it. Your ego side of you will never agree for you to have a routine you have never had before. The moment you introduce something new to your body to become a better you, your mind will create excuses to keep you in your old routine, but you simply need to make a decision to transform your mind, body and soul so that you can have abundance and success in your life.

If you made the decision to take control of your life, you can't explain the process if you don't introduce "<u>you</u>" <u>time</u>, and <u>working on you</u>. Furthermore, <u>exercising</u> is a <u>super-important part of releasing excess energy</u>, because otherwise you aren't creating the space for new energy to flow.

As an entrepreneur, not exercising creates a blockage around your aura. Exercising helps this. Even though you don't see why this will help, trust it will help your <u>organic growth</u>.

As an analogy, the Portuguese signature dish needs to have the right ingredients. For example, If it doesn't have potatoes, the whole thing just does not taste right. In the same way, all these steps for balancing the physical, emotional and spiritual side of yourself need to come together as one. They can't be worked on separately – sometimes this and sometimes that. All the steps need to come together in a combination of things.

It all has to come together as a signature dish.

BELIEVE
The Dream,
TRUST
The Process And
BALANCE
The Energy.

Chapter 13
Achieve Emotional Balance Through Stillness And Meditation

Appreciate Life

Be conscious of your "self" and grateful for being alive. Do it in the morning or when it's convenient. I recommend the morning, after you've had some rest. I recommend daily pauses throughout the day to bring yourself to realise you are living, breathing and creating. I do it every three hours, others do it every hour. Bring yourself back to you.

Attend meditation classes so you can live a life of extreme stillness to balance the extreme intensity of your entrepreneurial journey.

Practice Morning And Evening Gratitude

I have a morning gratitude routine of ten minutes where I acknowledge myself. I try to be calm, and connect to and release my thoughts. Say to yourself what are you grateful for. It could be anything.

Get into an evening gratitude routine so you can prepare your soul for the next day. Be thankful for what you have. Forget what you don't have. Ask for strength and positive energy from the Universe.

Bring Peace To Others

Have a five-minute conversation with somebody, and connect with that person to bring him or her peace. Connect with people who will contribute towards your connection with yourself.

Remove Yourself From The Frenzy Of It All

Sometimes you need to disconnect from the frenzy of reality. Take short countryside breaks from your everyday environment. Work in different places when you feel intensity in your current workplace. If you aren't productive throughout the day, shut down and take the day off. Change your routine. Take a different route to work or do something different.

Listen To Yourself

Listen to your intuition and your gut feeling and get the answers that are there. Follow up with timely action, before you talk yourself out of it. Truly believe that you have all the answers. Continuously ask yourself questions and talk to yourself. I genuinely believe we are a great source of genius and we simply need to find the answers within.

Identify Thoughts Versus Feelings

We operate on two systems – our ego and our higher self. We have been conditioned to make decisions using our ego. Everything you can explain the outcome of is an ego decision. Everything you can't logically explain, but you want, is your higher self. There is no logical way. Training yourself to identify both will give you clarity in your life and in business.

Connect with yourself through meditation and you will be able to identify which of the two you are basing your decision on. Ego equals comfort and higher self equals coming out of your comfort zone and potentially achieving what you want to experience. Basing decisions on ego will never give you a truly fulfilling experience.

You can have two friends, but find you laugh more with Mr Smith. The joke is the same, but you laugh more because of the difference in energy and how he expresses his joke connects with your inner self. It gels with your inner self.

Sometimes we get gut feelings and feelings of opportunity, but we get blocked by our mind. Why can't we do it? We give excuses as to why we can't proceed.

If you can understand how you feel and the decisions that come from current state versus your mind, you will be in a better position to take better decisions.

When you LOVE someone, it should be a feeling, not a thought process. If it's a thought process, you are battling against yourself. You need to understand how certain decisions are made so you can focus on the right thing – your ego self or your inner self.

Mastering yourself leads to becoming truly powerful, influential and magnetic in business.

Chapter 14
Reward Yourself

Pamper Yourself

You need time for you to switch off and feel whole again. The pressures of being an entrepreneur need to be remedied with time spent on you. You can try massage, reiki healing, sharing breakfast or coffee with friends.

When you do that, be present and feel intensely those moments that aren't intense but relaxing.

Reward yourself constantly so that you can "bribe" yourself with moments and memories you love. At the end of your life, you won't regret not spending more time at work, but you may regret not spending enough time doing things you love. Otherwise, what is the point of having a million pounds? Why have it, if you are not spending time with the people you love, doing things you are passionate about?

Do things that make you feel good in order to raise your soul vibration. As you feel excitement, joy, passion, love in your life, you become more in tune with what your purpose is in the Universe and you are more likely to attain inner balance and inner peace. This brings upon a feeling of centredness – where you have absolute clarity on what your next step is. Be patient, as this is not something you can rush. You need to be in flow for this to happen.

Holiday

Take time to refresh your energy by changing your environment so you can become more creative when you return to work. It doesn't have to be long-haul. It can be "You Time", whatever that means to you – a holiday with yourself. It can be a short break or family time. Identify what made you smile as a kid and try to experience that again.

"STILLNESS"
**Is Peace,
If You Can Handle Your Own Company.**

"VISION"
**Is Power,
If You Can Visualise The Outcome.**

"FORGIVENESS"
**Is Love,
If You Can Forgive Yourself.**

Find Peace

So, how do you find peace? Take time to forgive yourself for what you did and didn't do. Forgive others and become more appreciative of their existence. Try to connect on a deeper level to people. When you position yourself to connect with someone on a deeper level, it brings calmness. Take a retreat in line with a particular area of your life that you want to progress in or cure from.

Be open-minded about trying new ways of bringing peace in your life. You can try meditation, or crystals, such as amethysts, in order to bring balance and peace into your life. Identify what brings you peace and use those elements to feel balance in your life.

Be Open To Receive

In order to attract and create wealth and abundance in your entrepreneurial journey, you need to be open to receive what is being given or offered to you. If you don't accept and are not open to receive, the wealth will go somewhere else.

Allow Yourself To Be Sold To

Everything in life is energy. You need to be open to be sold to, so you can sell to others, also. Your energy needs to be in flow, so you can close more sales and attract more clients.

Speak Out Your Feelings

Write down your feelings and speak the truth – how you feel on a negative or positive level – and share your feelings with others, because you may just have an opinion that isn't what other people perceive of you. If you share it with others they may have a different view and opinion, which could heal you and help you turn your negative perspective into a positive.

Entrepreneurial Success Is A Signature Dish

Entrepreneurial success is kind of like a signature dish made up of many ingredients. They need to be timed well. They need to be prepared and nurtured well. They need to be quality organic ingredients. We need to trust that the outcome will be delicious. You need patience, as part of the signature dish.

If you believe you can be better, you can believe you have the inner power to create anything you want to create.

You need to have that belief. The meditation and the element of stillness will create a power that not many people use. Why aren't we using our inner power? Why are we relying on the physical? The external blocks our inner life – the real us. The real you needs to go through the real process of identifying who you are.

There are various processes you can adopt if you want to become a better "you", complemented by a spiritual way of living balanced with your inner self.

When you are balanced, you are aligned with your true purpose in life. You are able to create wealth, inspire people or follow whatever your true calling in life really is.

Follow the entrepreneur paradox and you will find your life will start to unfold in ways you could not even imagine.

NO LIMITATIONS, NO RESTRICTIONS Except The Ones You Choose To BELIEVE.

Summary

The Entrepreneur Paradox is a system for you to use to attract abundance, success and clients, and to create a successful business.

It is about the foundation that needs to be laid down in order to create a successful business.

What many entrepreneurs do is to build on an nonexistent foundation, by running on empty, by not taking time for themselves to refuel, by having poor nutrition and ignoring time spent with their family. So many entrepreneurs are chasing money and they wonder why it doesn't come to them, whereas others seem to have it easy.

Some entrepreneurs forget about themselves and then they wonder why their business or their life collapsed. They spin their wheels, trying to create success. However, when your chakras are blocked, you could be going to the same networking meetings and not meet the right people because your negative energy is repelling people rather than attracting them to you. When you build your business by focusing initially on the three pillars of wealth – which are the spiritual, emotional and physical, in balance – that is when you start to build a sustainable business.

I have prepared a special masterclass for you as I would like to help you stay on track on your entrepreneurial journey and also so that you can start practicing using these tools I spoke of in the book.

Watch the FREE masterclass here: www.sandroheitor.com/masterclass

Partner With Me

If you are an entrepreneur who wants to:

1. make a difference, or
2. you have a joint venture idea you would like to collaborate on, or
3. you want to collaborate in property

Watch the FREE video here:
https://www.trio-thedifference.com/property

I would be most grateful if you could leave a review on Amazon for me.

Hope to meet you someday!

You can subscribe to my social media channels:

Instagram: @keepingupwithtrio
LinkedIn: Sandro Heitor
Facebook: Sandro Heitor
YouTube: Sandro Heitor
Podcast: The Entrepreneur Paradox Podcast

Printed in Poland
by Amazon Fulfillment
Poland Sp. z o.o., Wrocław